Any other characters on stage during this song now leave. The an[imals] (or a group of them – two or more) step forward and address the audie[nce]

Animals:	We're not due back till later on,
	Just in time for the final song;
	But if we stay as quiet as mice,
	To watch with you would be so nice!
	And even in the funniest bit
	We'll try, our hardest, just to sit!
	And if we're moved to shed a tear
	We'll do it quietly, don't you fear!
	For now, 'bye bye', then, human friends
	Until the story nearly ends…

Any mice look flattered

All the animals sit at the foot of the stage and watch.

SCENE 2: NAZARETH

Narrators:	Long before the stable scene
	Our story first unfolds:
	A girl called Mary quietly works,
	And an angel she beholds!
	Although this was around about
	Two thousand years ago,
	It still would be a mighty shock
	For anyone, you know!
	But so that Mary wouldn't stay
	Afraid for very long,
	The angel reassures her
	As you'll find out in this song…

Song 2   The angel's song

1. *All:* Mary, you will always be
   Remembered in our history.
   There's something precious going on,
   So hear the angel's song.

Chorus
Gabriel: Hallelujah, hallelu!
   Heav'n has shined her light on you.
   God has seen your heart is true,
   And He has chosen you.
   Hallelujah, hallelu!
   Heav'n has shined her light on you.
   You will bear God's Holy Son,
   The Lord's Anointed One.

2. *Mary:* Why would God reach down to me?
   I'm just His servant, as you see.
   Forever I will sing His praise,
   And I am His always.

Chorus *All:* Hallelujah, hallelu!
   Heav'n has shined her light on you.
   You will bear God's Holy Son,
   The Lord's Anointed One.
Mary: Hallelujah, hallelu!
   All you ask of me, I'll do.
   When You speak, Your words come true,
   So I will trust, I will trust,
   I will trust in You.
   I will trust in You.

Gabriel: Peace to you.
Mary: God be praised.

The angel leaves.

Narrators: Mary is a special girl
   As no doubt you can tell.
   She thinks about these words from God
   And treasures them as well.
   She tells it all to Joseph –
   He's the man she's going to wed.
   He too accepts it as God's will,
   And this is what he said:

4

Joseph: I know the Lord will care for us
And for the baby, too,
But there's going to be a census
So this is what we'll do.
We'll pack up our belongings
And without too much delay,
We'll travel to Judea
And in Bethlehem we'll stay.
And there, when we have stopped to rest,
The baby will be due,
And I will love him as my own...   *(pause)*
Mary, I will stand by you.

They leave the stage to pack.

SCENE 3: BETHLEHEM

Mary and Joseph enter; Mary is heavily pregnant; they both look weary. Various innkeepers and inns are situated around the stage.

Joseph knocks or rings at each door, according to the lyrics.

Song 3   **Who's that knocking?**

Innkeepers and wives:

1. **Who's that knocking on the door?**   *With drum or woodblock*
   If you want rooms we've got no more!
   We're busy in here, we're so busy in here!
   A pair in your condition should have got here long before!

2. **Who's that ringing on the bell?**   *With Indian bells or*
   Every room's full now, can't you tell?   *triangle*
   We're busy in here, we're so busy in here!
   And every place in town is going to be full-up as well!

3. *All:*   **Who's that knocking? Can't you see**   *With drum or woodblock*
   Everyone here's rushed off their feet!
   We're busy in here, we're so busy in here!
   But if you're really desp'rate, there's a stable going free!

   But if you're really desp'rate, there's a stable going –
   If you're really desp'rate, there's a stable going –
   If you're really desp'rate, there's a stable going free!

Narrators: 'Desperate' they certainly are,
             For the time has nearly come
             For you and I and everyone
             To meet God's Holy Son!

SCENE 4: IN THE EAST

Narrators: We leave these folk for just a while
             To settle in their shed
             With animals and straw and hay -
             Without a feather bed!
             For in a land far, far away
             Three wise men we espy
             Let's watch them spot a big surprise…
             Let's hear their startled cry…

One wise man enters the stage with a telescope trained at the sky, and gives a big shout as he sees the new star.
Wise Man: Hey!!

The two other wise men enter the stage and do the same.
2 Wise Men: HEY!!

Narrators: There's a lot of 'hay' in Stable Story!
Wise men groan.

Narrators: Sorry!

Song 4   We are wise men!

Chorus
Wise Men: **We are wise men, we search for reasons!**
             We are wise men, we search for proof!
             We are wise men, we search for wisdom!
             We are wise men, we search for truth!

1.   **When we saw the new star in the skies,**
             We very nearly fainted with surprise!
             But after we had blinked and rubbed our eyes,
             We did what you should do if you are wise…

Chorus *All:* **We are wise men, we searched for reasons!**
             We are wise men, we searched for proof!
             We are wise men, we searched for wisdom!
             We are wise men, we searched for truth!

2. **When we saw the new star in the skies,
    We very nearly fainted with surprise!
    But after we had blinked and rubbed our eyes,
    We did what you should do if you are wise…**

Chorus   *kazoos*

3. *Wise Men:* **If you want to be wise girls and boys,
    When you've finished playing with your toys,
    Always search for reasons 'how' and 'why',
    And when you see the stars up in the sky,
    Remember you can find God if you try…**

Chorus *All:* **We are wise men, we search for reasons!
    We are wise men, we search for proof!
    We are wise men, we search for wisdom!
    We are wise men, we search for truth!**

Wise men: Quick, let's pack!

Two of them start to throw their belongings into bags; the third one meticulously considers and chooses and folds each item – the others tease him. Then they go to a special cupboard and pull out three gifts and hold them up to the audience.

Wise man 1: Gold!   *Choir say 'ahh' each time*
Wise man 2: Frankincense!
Wise man 3: Myrrh!
Wise men: Gifts fit for a King!

From off stage, loudly:
Herod: A KING?!?!

The wise men jump! A few loud chords or drum beats announce King Herod, and he sweeps in followed by four soldiers.

Herod: A KING, did you say?!?!

Wise men: No! Well, yes…

Wise man 1: Fit for a King, yes, but just a small one…

Wise man 2: Not a mighty King such as yourself, Herod! A baby King!

Wise man 3: We have found a new star in the sky, and our studies show us that it is the sign of a new K… K… K… leader sent from God for His people, you see…

Herod (*pauses, then, cunningly*):
> Oh, I *see*... Well, that's all right then, ISN'T IT?
> I know – you find him, then tell me where he is, and I'LL give him a present too – won't that be NICE?

He marches off stage, followed by his soldiers. (Can be accompanied by more piano chords or drum beats.)

Wise men (*sarcastically*):
> Yeah, *right*...

They walk off, excitedly, in the direction of the star.

SCENE 5: THE STABLE

Narrators: What a truly beautiful sight,
Despite the situation;
Mary holds the tiny child,
The hope of all creation.

Song 5   **Lulla, lullaby**

1st time   *Mary*
2nd time   *Instrumental*
3rd time   *Mary and Joseph (or everyone)*

1. & 3.   **Lullaby, lullaby.**
Do not fear, do not cry.
If I could just keep You
As safe as today…
But God has prepared You
A far greater way.
Lullaby, lullaby,
Lullaby.

Mary and Joseph settle the baby in the manger.

SCENE 6: A HILLSIDE

A group of shepherds are sitting chatting on a hillside, by a camp fire, at night. There are sheep around!

Narrators: On a hillside just near-by
Some shepherds watch their sheep.
When suddenly a light appears
And to their feet they leap!

A host of angels appear and praise the Lord:

Song 6   **Amen! Amen!**

The angels sing verse one to the shepherds; all sing the choruses. All sing the second time through.

Angels: **Come and worship your Messiah!**
Peace on earth, goodwill to men!
'Hallelujahs' and 'hosannas'!
We will praise Him, without end!
Singing 'Glory to the Father!'
Singing 'Glory to the Son!'
God has sent His Son from heaven,
To bring hope for everyone!

All: **Amen! Amen! Amen! Amen!**   *Angels raise hands*
Amen! Amen! Amen! Amen!   *and sway left to right*

All repeat song

SCENE 7: THE STABLE

Mary and Joseph sit together; Mary holds the baby.

Narrators: Finally our story takes us
Back to Bethlehem once more
Here we started, here we finish…
Come on animals – take the floor! (*They beckon to the animals*)

The animals – who have been watching the play – come rushing happily back on stage. Everyone sings, and the wise men (offering their gifts), shepherds, angels and innkeepers quickly arrive on stage during the song, joining in as soon as their acting allows.

Song 7 **Stable story, Christmas glory!**

All sing, in a tableau, to the exact music of song 1

1. **Stable story! Stable story!**
   Have you all enjoyed our play?
   We have seen God's Christmas glory
   In our presence here today!
   Come and worship Christ the Saviour!
   Lift your voices high and sing:
   Hallelujah, hallelujah,
   Hallelujah, Christ the King!

2. **Stable story! Stable story!**
   It's the ending of our play!
   We have seen God's Christmas glory
   In our presence here today!
   Come and worship Christ the Saviour!
   Join with us, now, everyone!
   For we know this stable story's
   Only really just begun!

   Yes, we know this stable story's
   Only really just begun!

Animals/narrators/whole cast:
   It's the most exciting story!
   It's in the bible for all to see!
   May the power of God's glory
   Touch the lives of you and me.
   Have a safe and peace-filled Christmas,
   Share God's love with everyone!
   Now if you clap us very loudly,
   Who knows, an encore may be sung!